WE
THE PEOPLE
GERONIMO

Library of Congress Cataloging-in-Publication Data

Rothaus, James.
  Geronimo.

  (We the people)
  Summary: A biography of the Apache chief who led one
of the last great Indian uprisings against the United
States Army.
  1. Geronimo, Apache Chief, 1829-1909—Juvenile
literature.   2. Apache Indians—Biography—Juvenile
literature.   3. Apache Indians—History—Juvenile
literature.   4. Indians of North America—Southwest, New
—History—Juvenile Literature.   [1. Geronimo, Apache
Chief, 1829-1909.   2. Apache Indians—Biography.
3. Indians of North America—Biography]   I. Title.
II. Series: We the people (Mankato, Minn.)
E99.A6G327   1987   970.004'97   [B]   [92]   87-24580
ISBN 0-88682-159-2

WE
THE PEOPLE
GERONIMO

APACHE WARRIOR
(1829-1909)

JAMES R. ROTHAUS

Illustrated By John Keely And Dick Brude

CREATIVE EDUCATION

GERONIMO

More than a million Indian people were living in North America when the white settlers first began moving westward across the continent. Of those million, none were better warriors than the proud Apache who roamed the arid mountains and desert lands of New Mexico, Arizona and Mexico.

There were many bands of Apaches. The Bedonkohe lived in the parched lands along the Gila River in Arizona. The men hunted deer, wild turkey, and sometimes buffalo. The women and children tended small gardens of corn, melons, and pumpkins. Most of the time, they were at peace. Their distant neighbors—the Navaho, Hopi, Zuni and Pueblo Indians—did not want to rile the smaller but tougher Apache.

In 1829 a boy named Goyakla —The Yawner—was born. His mother was the daughter of Chief Mahko. His father had come from the wild Nedni band, of Mexico. There was no way of knowing that this sleepy little Indian infant would one day become the legendary Chief Geronimo.

Like most Apache children, Goyakla was not tall. But he grew strong and brave, with a keen mind. His parents loved him.

Goyakla's mother taught him the secrets of Apache farming. His

father trained him to run very fast, to ride like a warrior, and to outfox the animals on a hunt. Life was good, and Goyakla was very happy.

All the time that Goyakla was small, he never saw a white man. But he heard stories of troubles brewing to the south. The Apaches in Mexico became angry when the settlers took over their land and their water. When the Indians raided the

white towns and ranches, the Mexican state of Sonora declared war.

The government of Sonora said it would pay 100 pesos for each Apache warrior's scalp. A white trader in Arizona named James Johnson decided to make some money. He set a trap for the friendly Bedonkohe Apaches — Goyakla's tribe. When the Indians came in peace to trade with him, Johnson used a hidden cannon to kill many, including the chief.

Sadly, the new chief—Mangas Coloradas—gathered all his warriors together. His words were clear and firm. "From now on," he told them, all white men must be our enemies."

The talk of war was exciting to young Goyakla. He longed to use the skills his father had taught him, and he was not afraid to die in defense of his tribe. But Apache custom said he had to wait until age 17 to become a warrior. By that time, most of the fighting seemed over. Mexico was going to sell the Arizona territory to the United States. The U.S. government wanted to make peace with the Apaches.

Goyakla married his childhood sweetheart, Alope. For three years, they and their people had peace. Life was good again, but not for long.

In 1851, the entire Bedonkohe band went south into Mexico to trade. But the Indians did not understand that the Mexicans were still at war with them. Mexican sol-

diers surprised and massacred the Apaches near Janos.

Goyakla's mother, his young wife, and their three small children were all killed. So were many other members of the band. The rest escaped in terror into the hills. Chief Mangas Coloradas led his sorrowing people back to Arizona.

Goyakla's heart was filled with grief and rage. His family had been taken from him—murdered! Now, revenge was his only thought. The chief sent him to the Chiricahua Apache band to raise an army. Chief Cochise agreed to join the fight against the Mexicans. The Nedni Apaches joined them, too. They vowed to fight together as brothers against the white invaders.

14

Goyakla was still a young man, but the chiefs of the three bands asked him to be their guide as they slipped into Mexico to take the warpath.

Goykala and his warriors rode their war ponies quietly through the night. The enormous desert floor became a shimmering sea of silver in the moonlight. The Apache ponies and their riders cast long shadows into the sagebrush, and Goyakla could see the eyes of curious jackrabbits glowing back at him.

Looking up at the night sky, he recalled how his wife and children had delighted in counting the stars together. Now, his family was gone—taken from him by the white soldiers. Goyakla's knuckles turned

pale as he clutched his rifle. Soon he would have his revenge.

The Indians came face to face with Mexican troops near Arizpe. Goyakla led the attack. In the terrible battle that followed, the Mexicans gave him a new name. They called him Geronimo. With enemy soldiers shouting his name, he led the Indians to victory.

In the years that followed, Goyakla became a famous raider, striking into Mexico from an Arizona base camp. Stories were told of his courage and daring. It was whispered that he never slept—that he went by himself at night to gaze at the stars and think. Even the Indians began to call him Geronimo. At long last, he married a woman from Cochise's band.

The United States was supposed to be at peace with the Apaches. American settlers came into Arizona, moving closer and closer to old Indian lands, but honoring the unmarked boundaries.

Geronimo was a member of Cochise's band, but he did not fight Americans—only Mexicans. For nearly ten years, the Chiricahua Apaches had peace.

Then, in 1861, a young army man accused Cochise of stealing cattle and kidnapping a white boy. He tried to arrest the chief. This started an Indian war.

Mangas Coloradas and his band joined with Cochise in fighting the U.S. Army. Geronimo was away, fighting in Mexico.

The Apaches attacked white settlements all over Arizona. In 1863 Mangas Coloradas was captured and killed by the Americans. Cochise became war chief of the entire tribe. Geronimo returned from Mexico and fought with Cochise against the army for nearly ten years.

Many times the white soldiers thought they had trapped Geronimo and his braves, but somehow the Apaches would always find a way to slip the trap. The Indian people, who had lived and fought in this land for a thousand years, were too clever for the soldiers.

Then, in 1871, the famous Indian fighter, General George Crook, was sent to put down the Apaches and make Arizona safe for white settlers. Crook was a cunning man who determined to fight the Apaches in their own way. He enlisted Apache traitors as scouts in his army. Soon, the white soldiers discovered and learned the ancient secrets of the Apache braves.

Outnumbered, the Indian bands had to surrender, one by one. In 1872, even Cochise and Geronimo gave up and went to live on a reservation.

The proud Apaches were told to become farmers. Many refused. Geronimo finally led a group of these "renegade" Apaches into Mexico. Not long after, Cochise died. The only strong war leader left to the Apaches was Geronimo. But even this great warrior wondered how so few Indians could ever stand up to so many white soldiers and settlers.

In his heart, Geronimo knew that the Indian way of life was now coming to an end, but still he fought on. He and his warriors resisted the whites in the best way they knew— by mounting a series of swift, furious raids and escapes. They were only a handful, but they were relentless.

Sometimes, when hardships overcame them, they would go back to the reservation for a short time. But then they would break out again. Year after year the raids went on. Once Geronimo was captured and imprisoned. But when he was set free, he went back to his old ways.

In 1885, General Croceived permission to pursue Geronimo into Mexico. His army, facing terrible hardships, chased the Apaches into the wild Sierra Madre.

The women and children in Geronimo's little band were suffering from the long pursuit. Most of the men now longed for peace. They were tired of hiding in the barren mountains.

Several times, General Crook offered to talk peace with Geronimo. Finally, in 1886, the Indian leader met with the American general. He agreed to surrender.

That night, a white troublemaker brought liquor to the Apaches. Geronimo began to regret what he had done. Shots were fired by drunken Indians and Geronimo thought the band was being attacked. He and a few other Apaches fled into the mountains.

When the U.S. government learned Geronimo had escaped, General Crook was recalled. General Nelson A. Miles took up the pursuit of Geronimo. He chased the Apaches all summer. Finally his forces caught up with the old warrior and convinced him again to surrender.

Geronimo said: "I will quit the warpath and live at peace hereafter." Then, surrounded by the U.S. Army, the Apaches marched north to Fort Bowie.

Though Geronimo was now nearly sixty years old, his face was

smooth, his back straight, and his eyes clear and bright. The U.S. government feared he might be able to lead young Indians to war again, if he was allowed to live on the reservation. A decision was made.

Geronimo and his people were imprisoned—first in Florida, then in Alabama. In 1892 they were sent to live at Fort Sill, Indian Territory. It was here that Geronimo died in 1909 at the age of eighty. Even in his final days, sparks of hope flickered in the Indian leader's eyes. He died, still dreaming that someday his people would be allowed to return to their beloved home lands in Arizona.

For a long time, white Americans believed Geronimo was an evil savage. Now he is known as a man of fierce courage who dared to fight for his land and people.

WE THE PEOPLE SERIES

WOMEN OF AMERICA

CLARA BARTON
JANE ADDAMS
ELIZABETH BLACKWELL
HARRIET TUBMAN
SUSAN B. ANTHONY
DOLLEY MADISON

INDIANS OF AMERICA

GERONIMO
CRAZY HORSE
CHIEF JOSEPH
PONTIAC
SQUANTO
OSCEOLA

FRONTIERSMEN OF AMERICA

DANIEL BOONE
BUFFALO BILL
JIM BRIDGER
FRANCIS MARION
DAVY CROCKETT
KIT CARSON

WAR HEROES OF AMERICA

JOHN PAUL JONES
PAUL REVERE
ROBERT E. LEE
ULYSSES S. GRANT
SAM HOUSTON
LAFAYETTE

EXPLORERS OF AMERICA

COLUMBUS
LEIF ERICSON
DeSOTO
LEWIS AND CLARK
CHAMPLAIN
CORONADO